oooh!
picasso

With thanks to GrandPatty for making Picasso
one of my earliest memories.
Gratitude as well to my family.
George Greenfield, and especially the Picasso family
for letting us share Picasso in bold new ways.

oooh! picasso

Mil Niepold & Jeanyves Verdu

TRICYCLE PRESS
Berkeley | Toronto

what is this?

I am water
falling
from
on
high

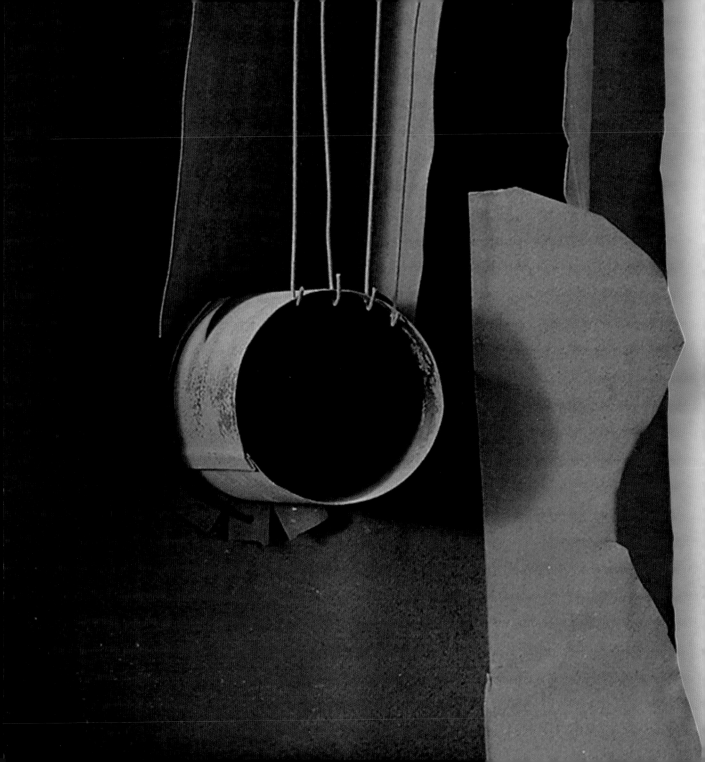

I am a tin moon
hooked to
the night sky

oooh!

i am
a guitar

and this?
what
is this?

I am a lollipop dreaming

I am a snail
hiding
inside a rose

oooh!

i am

a little girl

jumping rope

what is this?

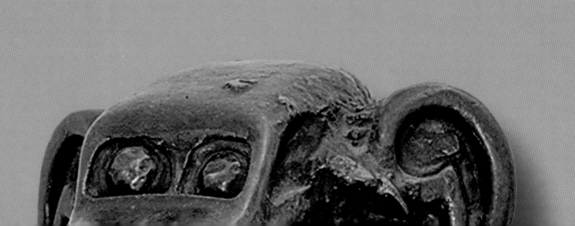

I am a robot playing catch

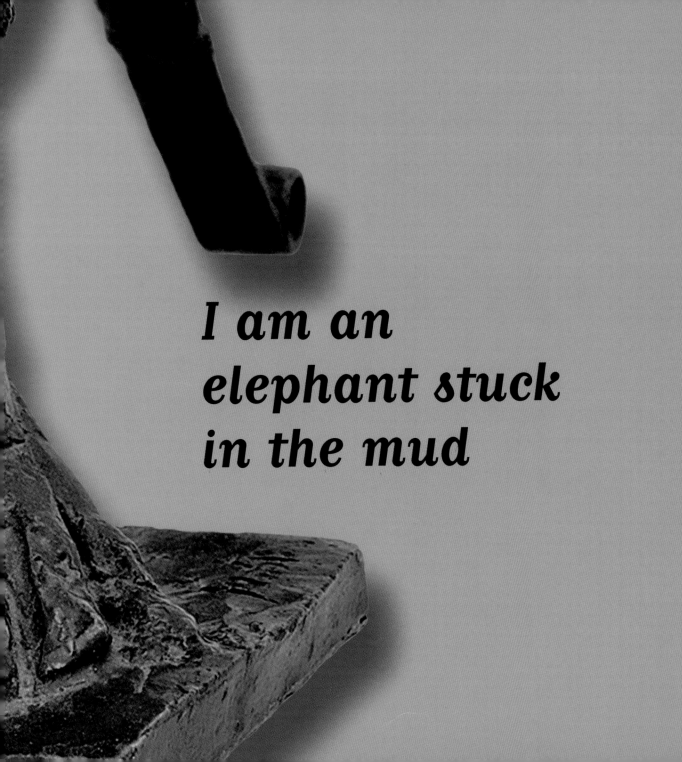

I am an
elephant stuck
in the mud

oooh! I am a baby baboon in my mommy's arms

what
is this?

I am a stairway

(where
do I lead?)

*I am
a paper mask
waiting
to be worn*

oooh!

I am another
guitar!

and
what
is this?

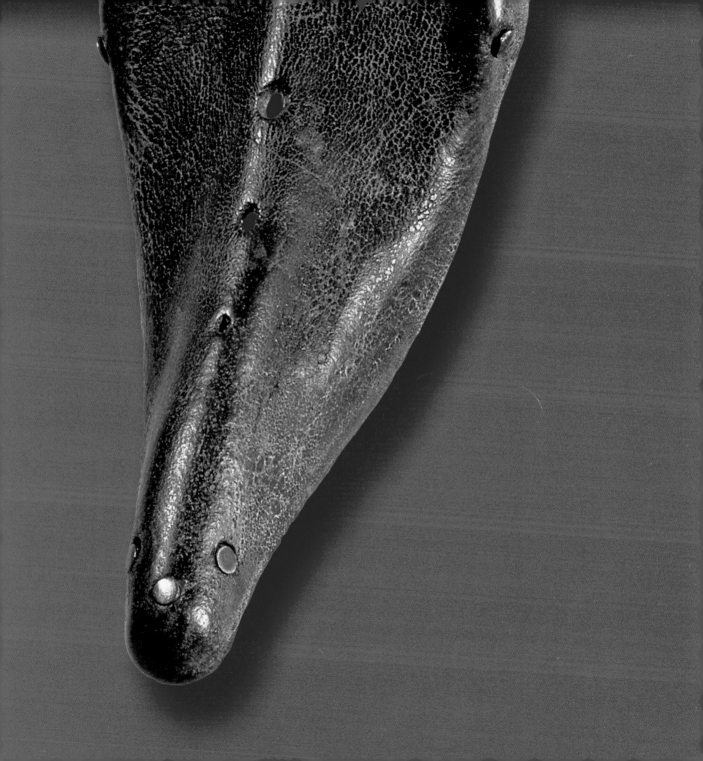

I am
a spider
doing
a handstand

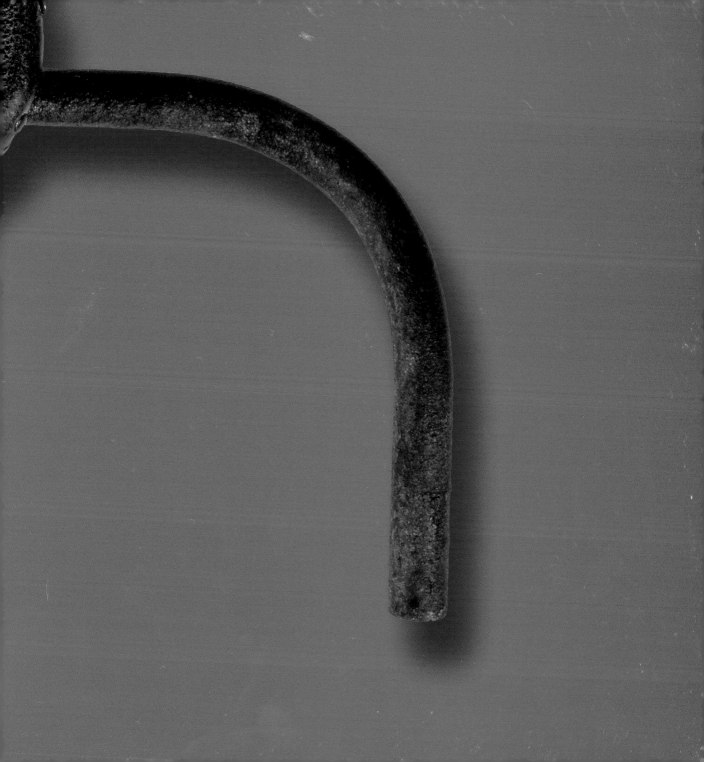

I am
a dolphin
leaping
through the air

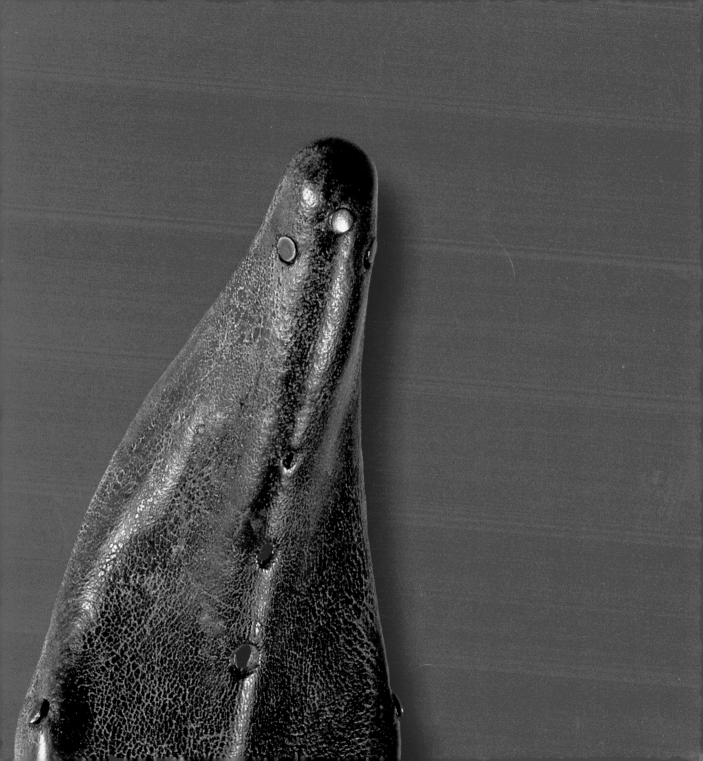

oooh!

I am a bull

(can your bike do this?)

oooh!

thank you
mister
picasso!

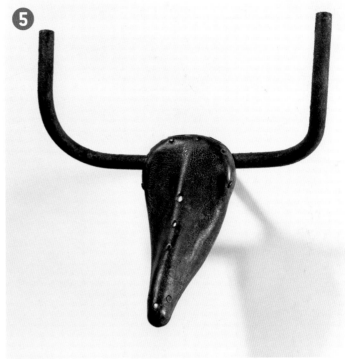

①

Guitar
Sheet metal
and wire.
/ 1912-13 /
Photo: Digital Image
© The Museum
of Modern Art

②

Girl Skipping
Wood, ceramic, iron,
plaster.
/ 1950 /
Photo: Réunion
des Musées
Nationaux

③

Baboon
and Young
Bronze from found
objects.
/ 1951 /
Photo: Digital Image
© The Museum
of Modern Art

④

Guitar
Mixed media:
paper, cardboard,
canvas, string.
/ 1912 /
Photo: Réunion
des Musées
Nationaux

⑤

Bull's Head
Assemblage:
bicycle seat
and handle bars.
/ 1942 /
Photo: Réunion
des Musées
Nationaux

Tricycle Press
an imprint of Ten Speed Press
PO Box 7123
Berkeley, California 94707
www.tricyclepress.com

Design by Jeanyves Verdu
Typeset in FarmhausITC, Matrix script, Conduit

Library of Congress Cataloging-in-Publication Data

Niepold, Mil.
  Oooh! Picasso / Mil Niepold, Jeanyves Verdu.
     p. cm. -- (The Oooh! artist series)
   ISBN-13: 978-1-58246-265-3 (hardcover)
   ISBN-10: 1-58246-265-8 (hardcover)
  1. Picasso, Pablo, 1881-1973--Juvenile literature. 2. Picture books for
children. I. Picasso, Pablo, 1881-1973. II. Verdu, Jeanyves. III. Title.

  N6853.P5N54 2008
  709.2--dc22
                              2008010646

First Tricycle Press printing, 2009
Printed in China
1 2 3 4 5 6 — 12 11 10 09